BE A WASTE WARRIOR!

CLEANING WARRIOR

GOING GREEN

by Claudia Martin

Consultant: David Hawksett, BSc

BEARPORT
PUBLISHING

Minneapolis, Minnesota

Credits: cover, © Mady70/Shutterstock; 1, © Shutterstock; 4, © Kanvag/Shutterstock; 4–5b, © Piyaset/ Shutterstock; 5r, © Nattapon Supanawan/Shutterstock; 6t, © Lovelyday12/Shutterstock; 6–7b, © Andriana Syvanych/Shutterstock; 7, © Monkey Business Images/Shutterstock; 8–9b, © Fevziie/ Shutterstock; 9r, © Shutterstock; 10–11b, © Africa Studio/Shutterstock; 11, © Dmitriylo/Shutterstock; 12, © Antonio Guillem/Shutterstock; 13, © Arne Hendriks/Flickr; 14, © Sarahbean/Shutterstock; 15, © BeaKendra/Shutterstock; 16–17b, © Fernando Avendano/Shutterstock; 17r, © Lopolo/Shutterstock; 18–19b, © Dragon Images/Shutterstock; 19t, © Rezacw/Shutterstock; 20–21b, © Zoe Cappello/ Shutterstock; 21t, © Olga Kovalenko/Shutterstock; 22, © Adam Gregor/Shutterstock; 23, © Isabel Sala Casteras/Shutterstock; 24, © Subbotina Anna/Shutterstock; 25, © Valery Evlakhov/Shutterstock; 26– 27b, © Switlana Sonyashna/Shutterstock; 27t, © Wertinio/Shutterstock.

Editor: Sarah Eason
Proofreader: Jennifer Sanderson
Designer: Paul Myerscough
Illustrator: Jessica Moon
Picture Researcher: Rachel Blount

Library of Congress Cataloging-in-Publication Data

Names: Martin, Claudia, author.
Title: Cleaning warrior : going green / Claudia Martin.
Description: Minneapolis, Minnesota : Bearport Publishing Company, 2021. |
    Series: Be a waste warrior! | Includes bibliographical references and
    index.
Identifiers: LCCN 2020031444 (print) | LCCN 2020031445 (ebook) | ISBN
    9781647476946 (library binding) | ISBN 9781647477011 (paperback) | ISBN
    9781647477080 (ebook)
Subjects: LCSH: Cleaning—Equipment and supplies—Environmental
    aspects—Juvenile literature. | Source reduction (Waste
    management)—Juvenile literature. | Environmental protection—Citizen
    participation—Juvenile literature.
Classification: LCC TD899.C58 M37 2021 (print) | LCC TD899.C58 (ebook) |
    DDC 363.72/8—dc23
LC record available at https://lccn.loc.gov/2020031444
LC ebook record available at https://lccn.loc.gov/2020031445

For more information, write to Bearport Publishing, 5357 Penn Avenue South, Minneapolis, MN 55419. Printed in the United States of America.

CONTENTS

The Battle to Save Earth! 4

Think Toothbrush! 8

Say No to Wipes 12

Swap Your Soap 16

Save Paper Towels 20

Ditch the Dish Soap 24

Eco-Activity: Make Your Own Shampoo 28

Glossary 30

Read More 31

Learn More Online 31

Index 32

THE BATTLE TO SAVE EARTH!

We all brush, wash, and wipe every day. But keeping ourselves and our homes clean can have the opposite effect on our planet! **Plastic** brushes, **single-use** wipes, and harsh cleaning products are all creating problems for Earth. But the good news is that a waste warrior can be green and still stay clean!

The Three Problems with Waste

Heaps of Garbage Much of our garbage is thrown into **landfills**. But when waste breaks down in landfills, it can harm our environment. Plastic can leak harmful things into the soil and air. Waste in landfills lets off methane gas as it breaks down. On top of that, the waste in landfills just sits there—stored up for a future generation to deal with. That is why waste warriors avoid creating waste!

Our waste piles up in landfills.

4

Wasted Resources Many cleaners used for washing laundry or dishes contain chemicals made from **oil**. The plastic bottles they are sold in are often made from oil, too. But the oil we use today formed over millions of years. And we are currently using oil at a far greater rate than it is made. Using this oil is taking away from our planet's limited **natural resources**.

Polluted Planet We create air **pollution** when we burn **fossil fuels** to power the factories where cleaning products are made and packaged. This makes our air dirty and releases **greenhouse gases** into the atmosphere. The gases, such as **carbon dioxide**, trap the sun's heat around Earth, increasing the temperature of our planet and contributing to global **climate change**.

Oil is often drilled from the rocks that lie beneath the oceans.

In some regions, climate change is causing droughts. These are times during which so little rain falls that rivers run dry.

The Six Rs

How can you become a waste warrior while keeping clean? Remember your Rs in the battle against waste. You don't need to be worried about how to start. Just do your best!

Refuse If you have a choice, say no thanks to extra packaging. Try a bar of soap instead of a plastic bottle.

A key skill in being a waste warrior is knowing which materials need to go in the trash and which can be recycled.

Reduce Try to cut down on single-use cleaning products, such as wipes, towels, and dusters.

Reuse Before throwing out cleaning spray bottles, consider whether they could be refilled.

Repair Try fixing broken brooms, baskets, and clothespins rather than throwing them away. You may need to ask an adult for help.

Recycle Try to **recycle** old cleaning packaging, so it can be made into something new.

Rot Put **biodegradable** materials in a **compost** bin so they will rot away.

When possible, choose packaging-free soaps, scrubbers, and sponges that are made from natural materials.

Wash and separate recyclable materials to get them ready for curbside recycling.

THINK TOOTHBRUSH!

Do you brush your teeth twice a day? Great! What may not be so great is your toothbrush's impact on Earth. About 99 percent of toothbrushes are made of plastic. And plastic is a big part of our waste problem.

Dentists recommend we change our toothbrushes every three or four months. This means we go through an awful lot of toothbrushes. Most toothbrushes are made in a way that makes them very difficult to recycle. As a result, most toothbrushes end up in landfills, where they will stay for at least 400 years! Brushes may also wash into oceans, where they are a choking hazard for fish, turtles, and seals.

If toothbrushes find their way into waterways and oceans, animals can mistake them for food.

What a Waste!

An estimated one billion toothbrushes are thrown away every year in the United States.

Many toothbrushes are made from polypropylene and nylon plastics.

Brushing with a clean toothbrush is essential, but what can a waste warrior do to reduce plastic toothbrush waste? Try brushing with something new! An alternative to a plastic toothbrush is a **bamboo** one. Because bamboo is a plant, a used-up bamboo brush breaks down much more quickly than one made of plastic. Plus, bamboo grows very fast, so it is much easier to keep up with the demands on this natural resource. You could also keep a lookout for toothbrushes made from recycled plastic and for toothbrush recycling programs.

Warriors Can Try:

Although toothbrushes can't go in curbside recycling, there are some mail-in recycling programs for used brushes. The plastic can be melted and turned into new products.

- Lawn furniture
- Playground equipment
- Bike racks
- Dog collars
- Yoga mats
- Brooms

Yoga mats are just one of the useful products that can be made from recycled toothbrushes.

Switching to bamboo toothbrushes will keep countless plastic toothbrushes out of landfills over your lifetime.

SAY NO TO WIPES

Wet wipes were invented in 1958. Today, more than 170 billion of these single-use cleaning wipes are used—then immediately tossed—in an average year. Wipes can clean surfaces, fingers, and faces. But what's wrong with wipes? Well, they pack plenty of problems!

If plastic wipes are flushed down the toilet into sewers, they can become stuck together and cause blockages. When sewers are blocked, they can overflow, sending wipes and other waste into waterways. Wipes that are tossed in the trash usually end up in landfills, where a wipe made of plastic will take at least 100 years to break down. Many modern landfills seal and store waste, but sometimes wipes leak harmful chemicals into the soil.

Every year, Americans spend more than $3 billion on wipes.

What a Waste!

During beach cleanups, the Marine Conservation Society found an average of 18 wet wipes on every 500 feet (150 m) of coastline.

In sewers, wet wipes can get stuck together with cooking fat and oils, causing blockages known as fatbergs.

The simplest way to reduce wipe waste is to clean up without them! Use soap and water on your skin. Clean surfaces with a reusable cloth and cleaner. Sometimes you might need a wipe. When that happens, look for options that biodegrade. These are usually made of plant **fibers**, which will rot away more quickly. And never flush wipes. Even most wipes labeled as flushable break down too slowly to keep sewers clear.

Warriors Can Try:

For wiping down household surfaces, try washing and reusing ripped old clothes.

- Flannel shirts are **absorbent** for soaking up spills.

- Cotton T-shirts won't leave behind a trail of fuzz when wiping.

- Old socks make good dusters— just put one on your hand to clean blinds, shelves, and books.

Flannels are a great eco-friendly alternative to wipes.

Reusable pads can be used, washed, and used again!

SWAP YOUR SOAP

When you wash your hands, do you rub a bar or press a pump? More than half of American families use liquid soap. But when the liquid soap dispensers are empty, they may create waste instead of suds.

The plastic bottles that hold hand soaps are often made of recyclable plastics. The problem with a liquid soap dispenser is that the pump head contains a metal spring and a mixture of different plastics, which makes it difficult to separate the parts for recycling. If you throw a liquid soap pump in the curbside recycling bin, it will almost certainly be tossed into a landfill.

It turns out that liquid soap bottles are not so clean after all! Studies have shown that these bottles can be breeding grounds for all kinds of nasty **bacteria**. Another reason to switch to bar soap, Waste Warrior!

What a Waste!

It takes 20 times more energy to make a bottle of soap than it does to create a bar of soap.

A pump seems like a simpler option for cleaning but it is far from clean or simple to dispose of.

To reduce soap dispenser waste, a simple suds swap can help. Switching the pump with a bar of soap eliminates plastic bottle waste. If you're feeling creative, you could even ask an adult to help you make homemade soap! But if you already have an empty soap dispenser, it doesn't have to go to the dump. Look for a soap refill. Then, when your pump soap dispenser is truly broken, unscrew the pump head and toss it in the trash before you put the bottle in the curbside recycling.

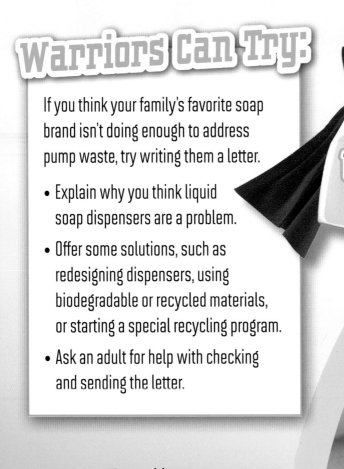

Warriors Can Try:

If you think your family's favorite soap brand isn't doing enough to address pump waste, try writing them a letter.

- Explain why you think liquid soap dispensers are a problem.

- Offer some solutions, such as redesigning dispensers, using biodegradable or recycled materials, or starting a special recycling program.

- Ask an adult for help with checking and sending the letter.

Try making your own soap by mixing glycerin soap base from a craft store with scented oils.

A lower-waste option is to refill a reusable soap dispenser with liquid soap from a bigger container.

VALUE REFILL

re-e
EVERYDAY
pH-BALAED
HANDWH

SAVE PAPER TOWELS

Paper towels are easy for wiping spills and drying hands. And they're made of paper, so they can be recycled just like printer paper and newspaper, right? Wrong! Paper towels are one of the few paper items that can't be recycled. So this kind of paper often goes straight to a landfill.

Used paper towels can't be recycled because they are too wet or **unhygeinic** to be sorted at a recycling plant. Also, paper towels are usually made of paper that has already been recycled. When paper is recycled again and again, it breaks down, making it harder to keep recycling it. Once paper has been recycled seven times, its fibers are too broken down to be used again. So manufacturers often use that paper to make items such as toilet paper and paper towels, meaning you couldn't use them again even if you wanted to. How can you help battle towel waste?

Paper towels are lightweight, so they can easily blow away from landfill sites.

The United States uses more paper towels than any other country.

What a Waste!

Including the paper towels used in public bathrooms, Americans throw away more than 3,000 tons (2,720 MT) of paper towel waste every year.

Try to use washable fabric towels instead of paper towels whenever possible. But when paper towels are truly necessary, think before you toss them in the garbage. What else can you do with your used paper towels? Since paper is a natural material, many paper towels can be put in a compost bin. Just be sure they aren't covered in cleaning products or grease. What if you don't have a compost bin? The good news is that part of paper towel rolls can still be recycled—the inner cardboard tubes. The tubes still have a few more turns to go in the recycling plant, and every little bit helps!

Warriors Can Try:

Although many paper products can go in the recycling bin, there are a few other exceptions that a waste warrior needs to watch for.

- Wrapping paper that is shiny, glittery, or has tape attached

- Hardcover books that are bound together by glue, which ruins the pulping process

- Paper coated in wax to make it waterproof, such as paper to-go cups

A waste warrior can use a fabric towel!

Paper towel and toilet paper tubes can be turned into gift wrapping and packaging.

DITCH THE DISH SOAP

Enjoy helping out by doing the dishes? Great! But did you know that the average dish soap does not help the environment one little bit? Most dish detergents contain a mix of chemicals that, in large quantities, can cause harm to animals and plants in our water.

We use a lot of dish detergents! Our **water treatment plants** try to remove the chemicals from the detergents that flow into our treatment systems. However, some still make it into our rivers and lakes. **Antibacterials** in the soap can harm living things in the water. They are particularly bad for algae, which are tiny plantlike living things that are food for some fish. Another key ingredient in any dish soap is a surfactant, which removes grease. Surfactants can damage the sticky coating that protects some fish from parasites and bacteria. A waste warrior can help deal with this problem.

Dish soaps may contain antibacterials, but we don't need them. If we clean thoroughly with soap any harmful bacteria is removed from surfaces.

Fish and many other creatures are dying because we have polluted our waterways with detergents and other chemicals.

What a Waste!

In 2013, the Environmental Protection Agency reported that 55 percent of U.S. rivers and lakes cannot support healthy plants and animals because of water pollution.

If they are not too expensive, look out for dish soaps that aren't as bad for the environment. Some soaps have fewer harmful chemicals and contain vegetable-based surfactants that break down in water more quickly, harming fewer animals. When washing dishes by hand, remember that a little goes a long way. You need only enough soap for bubbles to cover the top of the water in a thin layer. By using less dish soap, you are helping the environment and helping to save money, too!

Warriors Can Try:

When choosing household cleaning products, such as dish soap, consider these factors that can make products more eco-friendly.

- Packaging made from a biodegradable or recycled material

- Refills available so you don't need to buy a new bottle every time

- Natural ingredients, such as baking soda, lemon juice, vinegar, castile soap, or plant-based oils

- No unnecessary perfumes or colors

For a low-waste option, pour homemade dish soap into a reusable dispenser.

Ask for an adult's help
to make your own cleaning
products using natural
ingredients, such
as lemon juice and vinegar.

Make Your Own Shampoo

Many store-bought shampoos contain chemicals, such as parabens, that can find their way into waterways and harm plants and animals. Parabens help keep shampoos fresh, but they can damage coral reefs. A creative waste warrior can say goodbye to store-bought shampoo by making their own eco-friendly version.

You will need:
- An egg
- A pitcher
- A fork
- 1 teaspoon of honey
- 1 teaspoon of orange juice
- 1 cup of water

1 Crack an egg into your pitcher. Then, whisk it with a fork until the yolk and white are combined.

2 Mix in 1 teaspoon of honey.

3 Wet your hair, then put the natural shampoo on right away—it will not keep. Massage the mix into your scalp and hair. This shampoo won't form bubbles, so you'll have to do a good job of rubbing it on your hair. Leave it on for 5–10 minutes. The egg yolk mixes with the dirt on your hair and can then be rinsed away. Honey smooths the hair strands, making them look shiny.

4 Rinse out the mix with cool water (hot water might start to cook the egg!). Be sure to rinse well so that the mixture gets completely out of your hair.

5 Mix 1 teaspoon of orange juice with 1 cup of water. Pour this mix on your hair to replace any egg smell with a nice orange scent. Finally, thoroughly rinse out the orange mix so you don't attract bees!

6 If this recipe doesn't work for your hair type, ask an adult to help you find a different one.

Glossary

absorbent able to soak up liquid

antibacterials things that are able to kill bacteria

bacteria tiny, very simple living things that can make you sick

bamboo a quickly growing, tall grass with a woody stem

biodegradable able to be broken down by living things

carbon dioxide an invisible gas in the air that is released when fossil fuels are burned

climate change the change of Earth's climate and weather patterns, including the warming of Earth's air and oceans, due to human activities

compost rotted plants and food that can be used to feed soil

fibers threads or strips from which paper and cloth are woven, braided, or knitted

fossil fuel a fuel made from the remains of animals and plants that lived long ago

greenhouse gases gases that trap the sun's heat around Earth

landfills pits where waste is dumped and then covered by soil

natural resources materials found in nature, such as trees, water, metals, and oil

oil also called petroleum; a liquid fuel that is found in the ground and is made from the remains of dead animals and plants

plastic a material, usually made from oil, that can be shaped when soft, then sets to be hard or flexible

pollution any harmful material that is put into the ground, air, or water

recycle to collect, sort, and treat waste so it is turned into materials that can be used again

single-use intended to be used once, then thrown away

unhygienic not clean

water treatment plants facilities where wastewater is treated to make it clean